PLANT-TASTIC! GREEN!

HOW PLANTS MAKE FOOD

BY REX RUBY

BEARPORT
PUBLISHING

Minneapolis, Minnesota

Credits
Cover and title page, © yurchyks/iStock, © Adam Smigielski/iStock, © AlinaMD/iStock, © amenic181/iStock, and © ljubaphoto/iStock; 4–5, © Larry Doherty/Alamy and © oly5/Adobe Stock; 5, © Simoncountry/iStock; 6, © tiler84/iStock; 7, © ThomasVogel/iStock, © sbayram/iStock, and © domnicky/iStock; 8, © breakingthewalls/Adobe Stock; 8–9, © Iakov Kalinin/Adobe Stock and © KateLeigh/iStock; 10, © Barbol/Shutterstock; 11, © zoyas2222/Shutterstock; 12, © didecs/iStock; 12–13, © amenic181/Adobe Stock; 14–15, © omersukrugoksu/iStock; 16–17, © temmuzcan/iStock; 17, © gsdm/Shutterstock; 18, © Nirunya Juntoomma/iStock; 19, © Jacob Lund/Shutterstock; 20–21, © Iakov Kalinin/Shutterstock; 21, © Saddako/iStock; 22 Step 1, © ILYA AKINSHIN/Adobe Stock, © bgblue/iStock, and © phototropic/iStock; 22 Step 2, © s-cphoto/iStock; 22 Step 3, © ILYA AKINSHIN/Adobe Stock; and 23, © sakdam/iStock.

Bearport Publishing Company Product Development Team
President: Jen Jenson; Director of Product Development: Spencer Brinker; Managing Editor: Allison Juda; Associate Editor: Naomi Reich; Senior Designer: Colin O'Dea; Associate Designer: Elena Klinkner; Associate Designer: Kayla Eggert; Product Development Specialist: Anita Stasson

Library of Congress Cataloging-in-Publication Data

Names: Ruby, Rex, author.
Title: Green! : how plants make food / by Rex Ruby.
Other titles: How plants make food
Description: Minneapolis, Minnesota : Bearport Publishing Company, [2024] | Series: Plant-tastic! | Includes bibliographical references and index.
Identifiers: LCCN 2022058250 (print) | LCCN 2022058251 (ebook) | ISBN 9798888220436 (library binding) | ISBN 9798888222362 (paperback) | ISBN 9798888223581 (ebook)
Subjects: LCSH: Photosynthesis--Juvenile literature. | Plants--Juvenile literature.
Classification: LCC QK882 .R839 2024 (print) | LCC QK882 (ebook) | DDC | 572/.46--dc23/eng/20221209
LC record available at https://lccn.loc.gov/2022058250
LC ebook record available at https://lccn.loc.gov/2022058251

Copyright © 2024 Bearport Publishing Company. All rights reserved. No part of this publication may be reproduced in whole or in part, stored in any retrieval system, or transmitted in any form or by any means, electronic, mechanical, photocopying, recording, or otherwise, without written permission from the publisher.

For more information, write to Bearport Publishing, 5357 Penn Avenue South, Minneapolis, MN 55419.

CONTENTS

Time to Feed! 4

Roots, Stems, and Leaves 6

Thirsty Plants. 8

Getting Gas 10

A Light Snack .12

Cooking with Sunshine. 14

Green Energy. 16

Breathing with Plants. 18

People, Animals, and Plants 20

Science Lab. 22

Glossary. 23

Index 24

Read More. 24

Learn More Online. 24

About the Author. 24

TIME TO FEED!

On a sunny afternoon, a little caterpillar wriggles from one plant to another. It is looking for juicy leaves to munch on. The small critter isn't the only one feeding, though. The plants it's chewing on are busy making their own food.

Scientists think nearly half a million different types of plants grow on Earth.

ROOTS, STEMS, AND LEAVES

Plants make their own food that they use to live and grow. They do it using their roots, stems, and leaves. Roots are the parts of a plant that grow down into the soil. The stems connect what's underground to the leaves reaching toward the sky. All these parts work together to make food.

Flowers don't help make food. They make seeds that can become new plants.

THIRSTY PLANTS

To make food, almost every plant on Earth needs water. Plants use their roots to suck up water from the soil. Then, the liquid travels up the main stem of the plant. From there, it moves through thinner stems and into tiny **veins** in the leaves.

Plants also get **nutrients** when they take in water from the soil.

GETTING GAS

Plants also need **carbon dioxide**. This gas is in the air all around us. It enters the plant through tiny holes found mostly on the underside of the leaves. These holes are called **stomata**, and they can open and close as the plant needs.

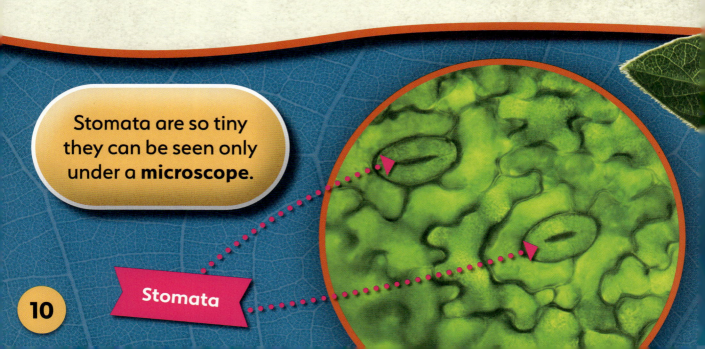

Stomata are so tiny they can be seen only under a **microscope**.

Stomata

A LIGHT SNACK

The final thing plants need to make food is sunlight. They **absorb** the sun using their leaves. Many plants can even turn so their leaves face the sun longer. Once plants have water, carbon dioxide, and sunlight, they have everything they need to get cooking!

No matter how leaves look, they all hold water, collect carbon dioxide, and soak up sunlight.

COOKING WITH SUNSHINE

Now, plants can start their most important job—making food! Inside their leaves, they use sunlight to turn water and carbon dioxide into a sugar. This process is called **photosynthesis** (*foh*-toh-SIN-thi-sis). The plants use this sugar for **energy** to grow and stay healthy.

The word *photo* means light, and *synthesis* means putting together. So, *photosynthesis* means putting together with light.

GREEN ENERGY

Photosynthesis can only happen with the help of a **chemical** called **chlorophyll** (KLOR–uh–fil). Chlorophyll can be found in many parts of plants, but it's mostly in the leaves. This chemical gives plants their green color, and it traps energy from the sunlight. Plants use the trapped energy to make photosynthesis happen.

Every green part of a plant has chlorophyll. It's even in some fruit that isn't ripe yet!

BREATHING WITH PLANTS

During photosynthesis, plants make more than just food. They also make a gas called **oxygen**. This gas comes out of the stomata on their leaves. While it is a waste product for plants, the gas is important for the rest of life on Earth. Without oxygen, people and animals wouldn't be able to live and breathe.

All plants make oxygen—from little houseplants to tall trees.

PEOPLE, ANIMALS, AND PLANTS

People and other animals can't make food the way plants do, but they still benefit from photosynthesis. When we eat plants, we take in their energy. We need plants to survive. But all a plant needs to make a tasty meal is water, gas, and plenty of light. Now that's really cooking with sunshine!

In addition to getting oxygen and food from plants, some animals make their homes in plants.

SCIENCE LAB
SUNLIGHT EXPERIMENT

A plant needs sunlight to make its food. Find out what happens when it doesn't get enough. Ask an adult for two potted plants with green leaves. Make sure they are the same kind of plant.

1. Place one plant in a sunny spot and the other in a dark closet.

2. Give both plants the same amount of water to keep their soil moist.

3. Check on your plants every three or four days. What do you notice about them? How do the plants look alike or different?

GLOSSARY

absorb to take in or soak up

carbon dioxide a gas people and animals breathe out that plants need to survive

chemical a natural substance

chlorophyll the substance in plants that traps sunlight and gives plants their green color

energy the power all living things need to grow and stay alive

microscope a tool scientists use to see things very close up

nutrients substances that plants need to grow and be healthy

oxygen a gas humans and other animals need to breathe

photosynthesis the process plants use to make food from water, carbon dioxide, and sunlight

stomata tiny holes in plants that gases pass through

veins stiff, narrow tubes that make the frame of a leaf

INDEX

carbon dioxide 10, 12, 14
chlorophyll 16–17
flowers 6
nutrients 9
oxygen 18, 21
photosynthesis 14, 16, 18, 20
roots 6–8
soil 6, 8–9, 22
stems 6–8
stomata 10, 18
sunlight 12, 14, 16, 22
water 8–9, 12, 14, 20, 22

READ MORE

Duling, Kaitlyn. *The Sun and Plants (The Power of the Sun).* New York: Cavendish Square, 2020.

London, Martha. *Photosynthesis (Discover Biology).* Minneapolis: Abdo Publishing, 2021.

Raij, Emily. *What Do Plants Need to Survive? (Science Inquiry).* North Mankato, MN: Pebble, 2022.

LEARN MORE ONLINE

1. Go to **www.factsurfer.com** or scan the QR code below.
2. Enter "**Green**" into the search box.
3. Click on the cover of this book to see a list of websites.

ABOUT THE AUTHOR

Rex Ruby lives with his family in Minnesota. He wishes he could make his own sugary food the way plants do.